What's in this book

This book belongs to

T0351515

_____

滑板不见了！
The skateboard is missing!

学习内容 Contents

沟通 Communication

说出房间的名称
Say the names of rooms

说说家中的房间
Talk about the rooms in a home

背景介绍：
浩浩的滑板不见了，他着急地想着家里能找到滑板的地方。

生词 New words

★	卧室	bedroom
★	洗手间	bathroom
★	书房	study
★	厨房	kitchen
★	客厅	living room
★	家	home
	花园	garden
	外面	outside
	里面	inside
	滑板	skateboard
	很	very

客厅很整洁。
The living room is very tidy.

文化 Cultures

中国的四合院
Traditional Chinese house

跨学科学习 Project

量度、绘画、描述房间
Measure, draw and describe a room

参考答案：
1 My bedroom is my favourite because I have all my things there and I can do what I want./I love the living room because I enjoy spending time with my family there.
2 Yes, I like his home. It is big and tidy./No, there are too many stairs in the house.
3 It may be in his bedroom/the living room/the kitchen.

Get ready

1 Which is your favourite room at home?

2 Do you like Hao Hao's home?

3 Where do you think Hao Hao put his skateboard?

故事大意：
浩浩心爱的滑板找不到了，他找遍家里所有的房间，最后在花园找到滑板。

参考问题和答案：

1　Hao Hao is wearing knee pads and a helmet. What does he want to do? (He wants to go skating.)

2　How does Hao Hao look? Why? (Hao Hao looks worried because he cannot find his skateboard.)

3　Is the skateboard under Hao Hao's bed? (No, it is not.)

huá bǎn
滑板

浩浩的滑板不见了，他很着急。

"很"即十分、非常，用在一些表示动作或者描写、修饰性的词之前，表示程度加深。如"很着急"表示着急的程度比较深。

wò shì
卧室

shū fáng
书房

xǐ shǒu jiān
洗手间

参考问题和答案：

1 Where does Hao Hao go to look for his skateboard? (He goes to the bedrooms, the study and the bathroom.)

2 Can Hao Hao find the skateboard in these places? (No, he cannot.)

卧室、书房、洗手间里面都没有滑板。

参考问题和答案：
1　Where does Hao Hao look for his skateboard? (He looks for it under the dining table in the kitchen.)
2　What does Dad say? (He tells Hao Hao not to worry and says that the skateboard must be at home.)

爸爸在厨房，他说："别急，滑板一定在家里面。"

客厅很整洁，里面也没有滑板。

参考问题和答案：

1 Where does Hao Hao go to look for his skateboard? (He looks for the skateboard in the living room.)

2 Does Hao Hao find the skateboard in the living room? (No, the living room is clean and tidy. There is no skateboard.)

7

lǐ miàn
里面

参考问题和答案：

1 What does Hao Hao remember? (He remembers that he skated inside his home a few days ago.)
2 Why was Mum angry with Hao Hao? (Because he skated in the living room and made a mess.)
3 What did Mum tell Hao Hao to do? (She told Hao Hao to skate outside.)

wài miàn
外面

浩浩回想起前几天他曾在家里玩滑板，把客厅弄得很乱，妈妈不高兴，叫他去外面玩。

"不要在家里面玩，到外面去。"妈妈说。

huā yuán
花园

"我知道它在哪里了，它在花园！"浩浩说。

Let's think

1 Hao Hao looked for his skateboard at home. Recall the story and number the rooms and places in order.

提醒学生回忆故事，观察第4至9页，注意各场所出现的先后顺序。

2 Which activity is more fun? What should the children wear? Discuss with your friend.

参考答案：

I love feeling the wind as I fly down the pathway with my skateboard. My friends also like to skate./I think cycling is more fun and it makes me healthy.

The children should wear elbow pads, knee pads and helmet for safety.

老师提醒学生，户外运动时，应该做好保护措施以避免意外发生，最好是在大人的监护下进行活动。

New words

1 Learn the new words.

延伸活动：
学生两人一组，一人随机说出生词，另一人指出图中相应的地点或事物，反之亦可。

书房

外面

里面

洗手间

卧室

厨房

客厅

滑板

花园

我很喜欢我的家。

2 Match the words to the pictures. Write the letters.

a 书房   b 客厅   c 厨房   d 洗手间

听听说说 Listen and say

第一题录音稿：
1 男孩：你在哪里？
　女孩：我在客厅。
2 男孩：洗手间在哪里？
　女孩：在卧室后面。
3 男孩：你的铅笔在哪里？
　女孩：在文具盒里面，在†

03 **1** Listen and circle the correct letters.

1 女孩在哪里？

a 卧室

(b) 客厅

c 书房

2 洗手间在哪里？

a 客厅后面

b 书房前面

(c) 卧室后面

3 铅笔在哪里？

a 书房外面

(b) 书房里面

c 洗手间里面

04 **2** Look at the pictures. Listen to the st

第二题参考问题和答案：

1 Where do you think Hao Hao's mum is going? (She is going home. She has finished grocery shopping.)

2 Who does the grocery shopping for your family? (My mum because she is a housewife./Sometimes I go with my mum to help her.)

d say.

3 **Role-play with your friend and answer the questions.**

学生仔细观察图片进行问答，尽量用完整的中文句子表达。

这个家很大，很好看，也很整洁，是吗？

是的，这个家很大，很好看，也很整洁。

爷爷在哪里？奶奶呢？

爷爷在客厅，奶奶在厨房。

谁在书房？谁在卧室？

女孩在书房，妈妈、爸爸和男孩在卧室。

洗手间里面有人吗？

洗手间里面没有人。

Task

先让学生画出自己家房屋的平面构造图及各房间的简单特征，再向同学介绍自己的家。
建议句式："这是……""我家有……""里面/外面是……""……很……"

Draw a floor plan of your home and introduce your home to your friend.

我的家有三个卧室，一个洗手间。客厅和厨房很大，花园在外面。

这是我的家。这是……

Game

参考聆听稿：
"我和姐姐在花园打球。""卧室里面没有人。""我家的厨房很大。""客厅在哪里？"

Listen to your teacher.
Point to the correct rooms.

爸爸去书房。

妈妈在……

……

Song

Listen and sing.

延伸活动：
学生唱到具体的地点时，需同时指向
图中相应的位置。

这是我的家，

外面是花园，

里面是房间，

上面是卧室，

下面是客厅，

家里还有厨房、书房和洗手间。

我爱我的家。

课堂用语 Classroom language

请再说一次。
Say it one more time, please.

写一写 Write

1 **Learn and trace the stroke.** 老师示范笔画动作，学生跟着做：用手在空中画出"弯钩"。

弯钩

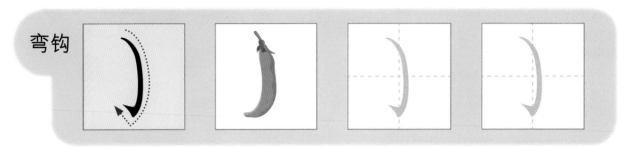

2 **Learn the component. Trace ⼧ to complete the characters.**
学生描完后老师做总结："宝盖头"表示房屋的屋顶。

⼧　窗　家　室　客

3 **Colour the roof red and) in the characters green.**
学生涂完色后老师做总结：这四个字都有"反犬旁"，
含有该部件的字多表示动物。

红色

猴　　狮　　猫　　狗

绿色　　　　绿色　　　　绿色　　　　绿色

4 Trace and write the characters.

下面两个字都是上下结构，提醒学生写的时候注意上方的部件写小些，下方的写大些。

家

、丶宀宀宇宇家家家

家 家

客

、丶宀宀宀突突客客

客 客

5 Write and say.

这是我们的 家 。

这是 客 厅。

汉字小常识 Did you know?

Some characters include a component that is placed on top and on the left.

Colour the top-left component yellow.

这些字的结构是（上左）包围结构。

房

厨

厅

后

在

黄色　　　　黄色　　　　黄色　　　　黄色

Cultures

1 Do you know what a *Siheyuan* is? Read and learn about it.

A *Siheyuan* is a traditional type of house with a courtyard surrounded by houses on all four sides. It is also known as a courtyard house. *Siheyuan* can still be found in Bejing.

四合院的"四"指东、南、西、北四个方向,"合"即这四个面的房屋围在一起,形成一个方正有院子的建筑。四合院的北面一般为正房(主人居住),东西两侧的为厢房(子孙们居住),南侧为倒座房(仆人居住),中间则是庭院。

老师可先简单介绍古代中国的各种房间,再进行练习。

2 Listen to your teacher. Point to the pictures and the words at the same time.

中国古代会客、活动的地方叫"堂屋",现在叫"客厅"。

厨房内煮饭需用柴木在灶头生火。

| 卧室 | 客厅 | 家 | 书房 | 厨房 |

书房和卧室的形式和现代差不多,但家具都是木质的。

Project

老师提醒学生先量门、床、桌子的尺寸，再将自己的卧室画在下方空白处，最后向同学进行介绍。可以从卧室整体及其内部物品等方面来描述。

Measure and draw your room. Talk about it with your friend.

你的卧室很整洁。

门很高，是红色的。

我很喜欢你的卧室。

床很矮，也是红色的。

我的卧室	颜色 colour	长 length	宽 width	高 height
门		____ cm	____ cm	____ cm
床		____ cm	____ cm	____ cm
桌子		____ cm	____ cm	____ cm

老师可要求学生先写汉字。再根据图画来填房间名称，一边填一边说出来。最后两人一组玩"捉迷藏"游戏：
一人在心中选定某一房间，通过"我（不）在……"的描述让对方猜测自己躲在哪里。

1 **Match the rooms to the words. Write the letters.**
Play hide-and-seek with your friend.

Trace the character.

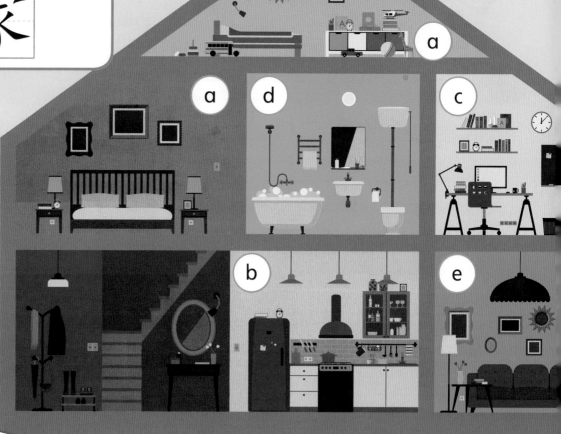

我在家里面。

我不在书房。

我也不在卧室。

我在沙发后面。

我在哪里？

a 卧室

b 厨房

c 书房

d 洗手间

e 客厅

你在……

2 Work with your friend. Colour the stars and the chillies.

Words and sentences	说	读	写
卧室	☆	☆	🌶
洗手间	☆	☆	🌶
书房	☆	☆	🌶
厨房	☆	☆	🌶
客厅	☆	☆	🌶
家	☆	☆	☆
花园	☆	🌶	🌶
外面	☆	🌶	🌶
里面	☆	🌶	🌶
滑板	☆	🌶	🌶
很	☆	🌶	🌶
爸爸在厨房。	☆	☆	🌶
客厅很整洁。	☆	🌶	🌶

Say the names of rooms	☆
Talk about rooms at home	☆

3 What does your teacher say?

评核建议：

根据学生课堂表现，分别给予"太棒了！(Excellent!)"、"不错！(Good!)"或"继续努力！(Work harder!)"的评价，再让学生圈出右侧对应的表情，以记录自己的学习情况。

21

分享 Sharing

Words I remember

卧室	wò shì	bedroom
洗手间	xǐ shǒu jiān	bathroom
书房	shū fáng	study
厨房	chú fáng	kitchen
客厅	kè tīng	living room
家	jiā	home
花园	huā yuán	garden
外面	wài miàn	outside
里面	lǐ miàn	inside
滑板	huá bǎn	skateboard
很	hěn	very

Other words

不见	bù jiàn	missing
着急	zháo jí	to worry
别	bié	do not
一定	yī dìng	certainly
整洁	zhěng jié	tidy
到	dào	to go to
不要	bù yào	do not
知道	zhī dào	to know

OXFORD
UNIVERSITY PRESS

Oxford University Press is a department of the University of Oxford.
It furthers the University's objective of excellence in research, scholarship,
and education by publishing worldwide. Oxford is a registered trade mark of
Oxford University Press in the UK and in certain other countries

Published in Hong Kong by
Oxford University Press (China) Limited
39th Floor, One Kowloon, 1 Wang Yuen Street, Kowloon Bay,
Hong Kong

Illustrated by Anne Lee and Wildman

Photographs for reproduction permitted by Dreamstime.com

China National Publications Import & Export (Group) Corporation is an authorized distributor of
Oxford Elementary Chinese.

Please contact content@cnpiec.com.cn or 86-10-65856782

ISBN: 978-0-19-082200-2

10 9 8 7 6 5 4 3

Teacher's Edition
ISBN: 978-0-19-082212-5

10 9 8 7 6 5 4 3 2